10 IMPROVISATIONAL TRUMPET ETUDES
by Jeff Coffin

ISBN 9781953622082
Copyright © 2021 by Jeff Coffin. All rights reserved.
No part of this book may be duplicated or shared without the permission of Jeff Coffin.

Also available online as an e-book.
Special thanks to Josh Karas for his assistance.
Layout and cover design by Robert Hakalski.
Engraving by Kyle Gordon.
Back cover photo courtesy of Jeff Coffin.
www.jeffcoffin.com/trumpet

WELCOME!

What you have here are my *Ten Improvisational Trumpet Etudes*.

I originally played and then transcribed them on flute (also available as *10 Improvisational Flute Etudes, 10 Improvisational Clarinet Etudes, 10 Improvisational Alto Sax Etudes, 10 Improvisational Tenor Sax Etudes, 10 Improvisational Piano Etudes*) and they work great for trumpet too!

I have provided free MP3 streaming and downloads at www.jeffcoffin.com/trumpet so you can hear and get a feel for the solos. These etudes are performed by five of the finest trumpet players on the globe: **Randy Brecker, Sean Jones, Jose Sibaja, Augie Haas, & Bill Fanning.**

If you want to play through them with backing tracks, which is best, I recommend getting the iRealPro app so you can change the various settings to your liking. These etudes are all based off jazz standards so the tunes are all in iReal. If this is already a familiar musical language and style for you, choose your own tempo and just start playing. If not, please listen to the examples and try to imitate how the etudes are being played. I recommend taking them quite slowly at first and eventually build them up to an excruciatingly fast tempo that makes your valves smoke from the friction!! Well, I DO recommend starting slowly.

As mentioned earlier, these solo etudes originated as improvisations I played on flute using iReal Pro. I recorded them into Pro Tools, transcribed my solos (tip: get the rhythms first if you're writing down solos), made some edits, put them into Sibelius, fixed the errors I made putting them into Sibelius, re-recorded them with the corrections and edits, and now they are ready to be played. Easy! :-)

I chose the chord changes to standard jazz repertoire that I thought would be familiar, beneficial, and fun to play. I think this book has something for everyone. Oh, and I named the solos just for fun. Some of these might be pretty challenging but it's always good to have things to work on that take some extra effort. I wouldn't want you to be bored.

In the places where there are two notes, you have the option to play whichever register is best for you. And if you listen in comparison to the woodwind etudes, you might find some of the trumpet phrases are broken up a little differently in regards to the phrase motion. They are all the same notes but I had to make some range choices along the way. I tried to keep it as close to the way I originally played it as possible though. It's very close.

The recorded tempos are for example only so it doesn't matter if you play them slower to faster than the recording when you're playing them on your own. Find tempos that work for you and that allow you to sound good and execute the material.

I hope you have a fun time with these and that you learn some things along the way. I know I did. Good luck!

Peace, JC

jeff@jeffcoffin.com
www.jeffcoffin.com/trumpet

TABLE OF CONTENTS

4-6 **Olive Mi** = All of Me
7 **Space Flies Like Star Pies** = Star Eyes
8-11 **Bluetude** = Blues (B♭ & C concert)
12-13 **It's The Little Things** = All The Things You Are
14-15 **Mrs. Kowalski** = Stella By Starlight
16-17 **The Answer Is Yes!** = Confirmation
18-20 **The Jones Tones** = Have You Met Miss Jones
22-23 **It's Only You** = There Will Never Be Another You
24-25 **King Of Leaps** = Giant Steps
26-27 **Where My Photos At?** = Someday My Prince Will Come

What makes these fine 'etudes' so interesting and fun to play is the fact they were originally improvised, then transcribed, by Jeff Coffin for woodwind players, so they get your 'trumpet fingers and mind' going into places we don't quite usually go!
Randy Brecker/Trumpet
Multi Grammy Winning trumpet LEGEND!

During the historic COVID-19 pandemic, many artists rose to the occasion to bridge the gap created in education by providing services and content for students, aiding in their continued progress in-spite of the challenges they've faced. Jeff Coffin's 10 Improvisational Trumpet Etudes, is a valuable resource for jazz education in that it provides harmonic, and rhythmic language in the form of beautifully written melodic etudes, that help students learn jazz standards forms, in spite of the difficulties presented by online learning and the inability to perform with others. This resource will help students grow during one of the most challenging periods in music education.
Sean Jones/Trumpet
Richard and Elizabeth Case Chair of Jazz/John Hopkins University's Peabody Institute, former Chair of the Brass Dept./Berklee College of Music, Jazz at Lincoln Center (2004-2010), SFJAZZ Collective (2015-2018), President of The Jazz Education Network (2020-2022)

This method is a "must have" in every musician's library. The approach to underlying chords and voice leading through improvisation by Jeff Coffin is masterful, player friendly; as well as helpful and thoughtful. A fresh and groundbreaking way to help players with their musicianship and improvisational skills. Bravo Jeff!
Jose Sibaja/Trumpet
Lead trumpet/Boston Brass • Associate Professor of Trumpet/Vanderbilt University

Simply put, I love these etudes Jeff Coffin has composed and adapted for trumpet! These etudes are musical, challenging, and lay great on the horn…A 'must have' for trumpet players of all levels.
Dr. Augie Haas/Trumpet
Harry Connick, Jr., The Maria Schneider Orchestra, The Vanguard Jazz Orchestra, The Gil Evans Project

I loved the challenge of playing Jeff's etudes. I found them to be melodic, rhythmic, and informative. I highly recommend his collection of etudes to any student or professional musician looking to advance their abilities.
Bill Fanning/Trumpet
Trumpet Solo Artist • Educator

OLIVE MI
All of Me

Comp. **Jeff Coffin**

SPACE FLIES LIKE STAR PIES
Star Eyes

Comp. **Jeff Coffin**

BLUETUDE
Blues in C

Comp. **Jeff Coffin**

BLUETUDE

BLUETUDE
Blues in D

Comp. **Jeff Coffin**

BLUETUDE

IT'S THE LITTLE THINGS
All The Things You Are

Comp. **Jeff Coffin**

-12-

IT'S THE LITTLE THINGS

MRS. KOWALSKI
Stella By Starlight

Comp. **Jeff Coffin**

MRS. KOWALSKI

THE ANSWER IS YES!
Confirmation

Comp. **Jeff Coffin**

THE ANSWER IS YES!

THE JONES TONES
Have You Met Miss Jones

Comp. **Jeff Coffin**

THE JONES TONES

IT'S ONLY YOU
There Will Never Be Another You

Comp. **Jeff Coffin**

IT'S ONLY YOU

KING OF LEAPS
Giant Steps

Comp. **Jeff Coffin**

KING OF LEAPS

WHERE MY PHOTOS AT?
Someday My Prince Will Come

Comp. **Jeff Coffin**

WHERE MY PHOTOS AT?

ALSO BY JEFF COFFIN

10 Improvisational Flute Etudes
10 Improvisational Clarinet Etudes
10 Improvisational Alto Sax Etudes
10 Improvisational Tenor Sax Etudes
10 Improvisational Piano Etudes
The Road Book
The Saxophone Book (1-3)
Jeff Coffin & the Mu'tet Play-Along
The Articulate Jazz Musician (w/Caleb Chapman)

Available at **www.jeffcoffin.com**

www.ingramcontent.com/pod-product-compliance
Lightning Source LLC
Chambersburg PA
CBHW081312070526
44578CB00006B/854